iMath
Readers

Stir It Up:
Mixing Decimals

by Renata Brunner-Jass

Content Consultant
David T. Hughes
Mathematics Curriculum Specialist

NORWOOD HOUSE PRESS
Chicago, IL

Norwood House Press
PO Box 316598
Chicago, IL 60631

For information regarding Norwood House Press, please visit our website at
www.norwoodhousepress.com or call 866-565-2900.

Special thanks to: Heidi Doyle
Production Management: Six Red Marbles
Editors: Linda Bullock and Kendra Muntz
Printed in Heshan City, Guangdong, China. 208N—012013

Library of Congress Cataloging–in-Publication Data

Brunner-Jass, Renata.

Stir it up: mixing decimals/by Renata Brunner-Jass; content consultant
David Hughes, mathematics curriculum specialist.
pages cm.—(iMath)

Audience: 10-12
Audience: Grade 4 to 6

Summary: "The mathematical concepts of money, percentages, and decimals
are introduced as children plan for a lemonade stand using the distributive
property and algorithms. Readers learn about sales tax, adding and subtracting
decimals, and profits through different scenarios. Includes a discover activity,
history connection, and mathematical vocabulary introduction"—Provided
by publisher.

Includes bibliographical references and index.

ISBN 978-1-59953-568-5 (library edition: alk. paper)
ISBN 978-1-60357-537-9 (ebook)

1. Decimal fractions—Juvenile literature. 2. Addition—Juvenile literature.
3. Subtraction—Juvenile literature. I. Title.

QA117.B78 2013
513.2'11—dc23
2012023953

CONTENTS

Note to Caregivers:

Throughout this book, many questions are posed to the reader. Some are open-ended and ask what the reader thinks. Discuss these questions with your child and guide him or her in thinking through the possible answers and outcomes. There are also questions posed which have a specific answer. Encourage your child to read through the text to determine the correct answer. Most importantly, encourage answers grounded in reality while also allowing imaginations to soar. Information to help support you as you share the book with your child is provided in the back in the **Additional Notes** section.

Bold words are defined in the glossary in the back of the book.

An Inspiration

Aleta sat with her family one spring evening. She was flipping through a family scrapbook. She came to a black-and-white photo. "Dad, I forget, what was the story behind this picture?" Aleta said.

"That's Grandma and her brother. The picture was used in a newspaper article one summer," said Aleta's dad.

"A lemonade stand? That gives me a great idea!" Aleta shouted.

"What?" asked Maddie, Aleta's sister.

"I know what to get Grandma for her birthday! And I want to earn the money to pay for it."

"Yes! I want to hand out lemonade! And take people's money!" said Marc, Aleta's brother.

Their parents looked thoughtful. Then Mom said, "Sure. But you need a plan, like I do for my business. You've got a month before school's out. That gives you time to figure out the cost of supplies and how much you'll charge. Okay?"

"Sure! I can do that," Aleta said. "And I can put the math I've learned this year to good use."

Aleta got up to search for paper and a pencil. "I have a lot to think about and a lot to do," she said. "I think I'll start by practicing my **operation** skills."

iMath IDEAS

How Do We Multiply This?

Aleta was comfortable performing operations of addition and subtraction. But this seemed like a good time to review what she had learned about multiplying, especially multiplying **decimal numbers**.

She recalled that in a decimal number, the **place values** to the right of the **decimal point** stand for parts of a whole, or a fraction, in the **base ten system**. The base ten system is a system of writing numbers in which each digit in a number has ten times the value of the digit to its right.

Idea 1: Rewrite decimal numbers as fractions. Because the place values to the right of the decimal point in a decimal number represent parts of a whole, any decimal number can be rewritten as a fraction. For example, say a bag of lemons weighs 2.3 pounds. The 3 in 2.3 represents three tenths, or $\frac{3}{10}$.

Now, say Aleta wants 3 times as many pounds. She can multiply 2.3 by 3 by rewriting both **factors** as fractions.

$$2.3 \times 3 = \frac{23}{10} \times 3 = \frac{23}{10} \times \frac{3}{1}$$

Next, she multiplies the **numerators**. Numerators are the number of equal parts that a fraction describes. They are written above the line in a fraction.

Then, Aleta multiplies the **denominators**. Denominators are the total number of equal parts in the whole. They are written below the line in a fraction.

$$\frac{23}{10} \times \frac{3}{1} = \frac{69}{10}$$

Now, she can rewrite the product as a decimal number: $\frac{69}{10} = ?$

Idea 2: Use partial products to multiply. Say Aleta needs to multiply 2.3 pounds by a price of $3.80. She can use grid paper to model **partial products**.

Each bold border around a square on the paper represents an area of 1. And each square contains 100 smaller squares, or units. So, each smaller square within the whole square represents $\frac{1}{100}$, or 0.01.

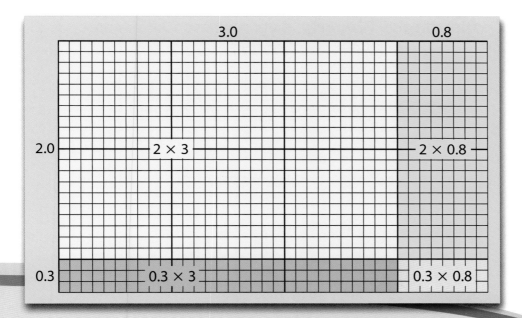

Each area of the grid is shaded a different color. Each of those areas represents a partial product.

$$(2 \times 3 = 6) + (2 \times 0.8 = 1.6) + (3 \times 0.3 = 0.9) + (0.3 \times 0.8 = 0.24) = ?$$

Add the partial products together to find your answer. How much will the lemons cost?

Idea 3: Use the Distributive Property to multiply. Say Aleta wants to buy a bowl to hold lemons at the lemonade stand. The bowl costs $3.85 plus 6% tax.

To find 6% of $3.85, she multiplies the dollar amount by the percent amount. First, she rewrites 6% as a decimal number:

$$6\% = \frac{6}{100} = 0.06$$

To use the **Distributive Property**, Aleta rewrites $3.85 as an addition sentence. She pays close attention to place values.

$$3.85 = 3 + 0.8 + 0.05$$

Next, she distributes the amount of tax, or 0.06, across the **addends**: $3 + 0.8 + 0.05$.

$$0.06\,(3 + 0.8 + 0.05) = (0.06 \times 3) + (0.06 \times 0.8) + (0.06 \times 0.05) = (0.18) + (0.048) + (0.003)$$

Aleta adds the **products** to find her answer. A product is the result of multiplying two or more factors, or numbers. What is 6% of $3.85? When Aleta rounds the answer to the nearest cent, the product is $0.23. Next, she adds the tax to the cost of the bowl to find the total cost.

$$\$3.85 + \$0.23 = \$?$$

Idea 4: Use an algorithm to multiply. An **algorithm** is a standard step-by-step method for solving a problem. The algorithm for multiplying decimal numbers is much the same as the algorithm for multiplying whole numbers.

Aleta practices using an algorithm to multiply 2.3 pounds of lemons by 3. She starts by stacking the factors, carefully aligning the factors to the right.

Then, she multiplies the decimal numbers as she would multiply whole numbers, beginning with the digit in the "ones" place in the bottom factor, or 3.

After finding the product, Aleta counts the number of digits in each factor that are to *the right of the decimal point.* In this case, there is one digit to the right of the decimal number.

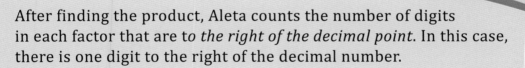

$$
\begin{array}{r}
2.3 \\
\times\ \ 3 \\
\hline
6.9
\end{array}
$$

2.3 ← **There is one digit to the right of the decimal point.**

↑ **Aleta starts at the far right. She counts 1 place to the left and inserts a decimal point.**

What is 2.3 × 3?

Empty the Piggy Bank

Imagine you are planning to run a lemonade stand. You know you are going to be working with dollar amounts, which means calculating with decimal numbers.

Like Aleta, you may want to practice multiplying decimal numbers.

Play with a friend. To start, put a collection of dollar bills and coins in a paper bag. Use play or real money.

On your turn, pull dollars and coins from the bag without looking. Count your total. Write this amount as a factor. Then, repeat the action.

Multiply the factors to find a product.

Decide which method you will use to multiply:

- rewriting the numbers as fractions
- modeling partial products
- using the Distributive Property
- using the algorithm, or standard step-by-step method

Use a calculator to check your work.

Give yourself one point for a correct answer. Then, let your friend take a turn.

The first person to earn 15 points wins the game.

Starting from Scratch

Aleta listed things she'd need to make lemonade. They were lemons, sugar, and water. But how much of each would she need to make one batch of lemonade? She wasn't sure.

Aleta had made lemonade with Grandma many times. She remembered that her parents had a box of Grandma's **recipes**. She thought she might find Grandma's lemonade recipe in there. And she did! It was a short list.

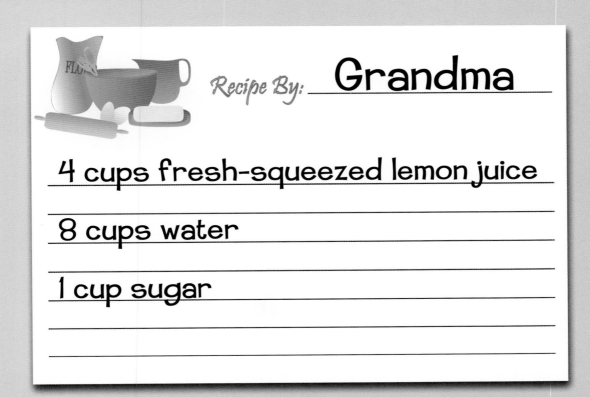

Recipe By: **Grandma**

4 cups fresh-squeezed lemon juice

8 cups water

1 cup sugar

After reading her grandmother's recipe, Aleta knew how much of each **ingredient** she needed to make one batch. They could use tap water instead of bottled water. That would save money.

They also had lemon trees in their yard. But those lemons wouldn't be ripe in time to start the lemonade stand. So, she knew they'd have to buy lemons and sugar.

 Did You Know?

In 1908, Frank Meyer, an employee of the United States Agricultural Department, returned from China in 1908 with a very small lemon tree, which came to be called the Meyer Lemon tree. This small tree grew in popularity until a virus that attacked the trees was discovered in the 1940s. To protect other kinds of lemon trees, the Meyer Lemon trees were banned. That changed in 1970, when the virus-free Improved Meyer Lemon tree was introduced. The tree has regained its popularity, as home owners enjoy growing lemons indoors.

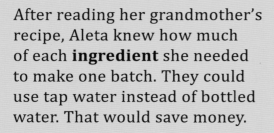

The next morning, Aleta and her dad went to the supermarket. She wanted to find out what some items would cost.

Lemons were priced at 80 cents per pound.

"Dad, do you know how much juice is in one lemon?"

"No, I don't."

"Okay," Aleta said, "I'm going to get some lemons so I can figure that out. Then I can figure out how many lemons I need for each batch of lemonade."

Aleta put some lemons on the scale. Four lemons weighed 1.1 pounds all together. If the lemons cost $0.80 per pound, what was the price of the lemons?

Rewrite the decimal numbers as fractions. Then, multiply.

How Much Juice?

When they got home, Aleta got out the juicer. Her dad helped her slice each lemon in half. Then, she juiced each half. She got about a quarter cup, or 0.25 cup, of juice from each lemon.

So, the juice of four lemons filled one cup. And together, four lemons weighed about 1.1 pounds.

Aleta looked at the recipe again. The recipe called for four cups of lemon juice for one batch of lemonade. So, she needed four times as many pounds of lemons. How many pounds of lemons did she need in all? 1.1 pounds × 4 = ?

Use graph paper to model and solve the problem.

Aleta wanted to test the lemonade to be sure the taste was perfect.

She and her dad went to the grocery store to buy the lemons she needed to make one batch. The lemons sold for $0.80 per pound.

Lemons—4.4 pounds
$0.80 per pound

How much did Aleta spend to buy lemons for one batch of lemonade? Use partial products to find the answer.

$$(4 \times 0.8) + (0.4 \times 0.8)$$

Aleta made a batch of lemonade as soon as she returned home. The whole family came in to taste. As Aleta poured the lemonade, Pooka wandered into the kitchen, too. He sniffed at some squeezed lemons that had fallen to the floor. The kitten froze. Then, he stood on two legs and hissed. All the while, he stared at the smelly objects on the floor.

"Poor Pooka!" said Marc as the kitten raced out of the kitchen.

Brainstorming

Aleta brainstormed some more. She listed everything she could think of that they might need for the lemonade stand.

They had many things around the house. There was water for the lemonade and making ice. There was some scrap wood to build the stand. And there were juicers and containers to make and store the lemonade.

She really only needed to buy lemons, sugar, and serving cups. Then, she thought, "Poster board!" They needed something to make a sign for the stand.

Aleta and her family stopped by an art supply store to find poster board. Maddie and Marc wanted bright yellow board to go with all the lemons. But the store was out of yellow. They bought a white board instead.

The price for the poster board was $2.00. At the cash register, 6% sales tax was added.

Remember that 6% means 6 out of 100 parts. In fraction form, you can write that as $\frac{6}{100}$, or six hundredths. In decimal form, six hundredths is 0.06.

Now that you know that 6% can be written as 0.06, you can figure out the tax on the poster board.

$$2.00 \times 0.06$$

What is the total sales tax on the poster board? Use the Distributive Property to find the answer.

What is the total cost of the board including the tax?

Supplies and Servings

The next day, Aleta figured out how much it would cost to buy the sugar she needed to make each batch of lemonade.

The sugar she planned to buy cost $3.99 for a 5-pound bag. Her recipe required 1 cup of sugar per batch of lemonade. Her mom helped her search for information on the Internet. She found that a 5-lb. bag of sugar contains approximately 11 cups of sugar.

Aleta divided $3.99 by 11 to find the cost of 1 cup of sugar. She calculated that 1 cup of sugar would cost about 36 cents. She used multiplication to check her math.

Was Aleta's result of 36¢ per cup a good **estimate**?

Use an algorithm to multiply the factors 0.36 and 11.

One cup of lemonade, Aleta decided, would be one serving. So, she needed to buy paper cups that could each hold one cup of liquid.

She found a package of 50 cups for $5.00. What was the cost after adding 6% sales tax? Remember, $6\% = \frac{1}{100} = 0.06$.

 Did You Know?

Scientists found that in one year, loggers cut down 9.4 million trees to make 23 billion paper cups. That's the number of cups people in the U.S. used that year.

It takes energy to turn wood into paper. Paper-cup companies used enough energy to power 77,000 homes. And they used 5.7 billion gallons of water. That's enough water to fill 8.5 Olympic sized swimming pools.

What happened to the cups when people were finished with them? They were thrown away. The result was 363 million pounds of solid waste.

Next, Aleta, Marc, and Maddie had to decide how much they would sell lemonade for.

In the picture of her grandmother as a girl, the sign read 5 cents per cup. She was certain that would be too little now. With some more Internet research, they decided that 50¢ would be a good price to ask.

If they sold 16 servings per batch, and charged $0.50 per serving, how much would they collect for selling a full batch of lemonade? How will you find out?

Aleta hadn't calculated the total cost of making one batch of lemonade yet. But an estimate of $5.00 seemed reasonable. If she were right, how much **profit** would Aleta make with one batch of lemonade?

Aleta calculated the real cost of making one batch of lemonade.

Lemons $3.52
Sugar $0.36
Cups $1.60

Then, she calculated 6% sales tax on the cups. Remember, $6\% = \frac{6}{100} = 0.06$.

What is the total cost for making one batch of lemonade, including the sales tax on the cups? (Hint: Round the tax amount to the nearest penny.)

Maddie interrupted Aleta to tell her about a clapping game about lemonade that she and Mom had found on the Internet. She was eager to show Aleta what she had learned. So, Aleta played along, and Maddie chanted the words as they clapped.

Lemonade, crunchy ice
Beat it once, beat it twice.
Lemonade, crunchy ice
Beat it once, beat it twice.
Turn around, touch the ground,
FREEZE.

Actually, Aleta thought to herself, Maddie's clapping game might bring in more young customers to the lemonade stand. She made that note on her business plan.

A Pink Possibility

The end of the school year was approaching. Only a couple of weeks to go!

One day, Marc brought home a book from the school library. He ran to find Aleta.

"Aleta! Guess what I found! This book has a story about *pink lemonade* in it! Listen!"

They learned that there are several stories about the invention of pink lemonade. Marc read, "One newspaper wrote that Henry E. 'Sanchez' Allott invented the drink when he was selling lemonade at a circus. He accidentally dropped some bright red cinnamon candies in a batch of lemonade, which turned it pink. There are several other stories that claim that one person or another, also working in a circus or carnival, served lemonade into which a horse rider's red tights had fallen. The dye from the tights made the lemonade pink, and the inventor served it anyway!"

Aleta responded to her brother's story. "Ewww!" she said.

They laughed about it. But then she wondered if they should sell pink lemonade at their stand. It would mean buying another ingredient. But first she had to figure out how much profit they could make with each batch they sold of plain lemonade. That is, after she paid all the costs per batch, how much would be left over?

She knew they could take in $8.00 per batch of lemonade. That is, if they sold all of it. She had calculated that it would cost about $5.50 per batch for supplies.

With the current price of lemons, what would be their profit per batch?

What's the Word?

Sometimes, English speakers use the word *lemon* to describe something that doesn't work like it should. For example, a new car is expected to run perfectly. But if someone buys a new car, and the new car has lots of problems that require fixing, the owner may call it "a lemon." The owner can also use state "lemon laws" to hold the car-maker responsible.

Building a Lemonade Stand

Aleta felt discouraged when she took her estimates to her parents. By now, she was getting attached to the idea of the lemonade stand and selling homemade lemonade. She almost didn't care about how much they'd make. But it seemed like a lot of work for little financial return.

"Well, we're really lucky to have lemon trees growing in our back yard. You can wait until the store lemons go down in price, or our lemons ripen. It just means starting a little later in summer on the lemonade stand," her father suggested.

"I agree," said Aleta. "But we could start building the stand, couldn't we?"

"Sure," said her mom, who had stacked some wood left over from a fencing project. "I'll show you the boards you can choose from."

Most of the spare wood pieces were all the same length. Aleta and her mom decided these would work for the top and front of their lemonade stand.

She wanted to make sure the counter was low enough for Marc and Maddie to work at. And some wood would need to be cut shorter for the sides.

Aleta measured the boards she'd picked to use for the stand. The planks were all the same length. They each measured 1.22 meters (m). She decided the pieces for the side of the lemonade stand should be 0.75 m long. How much will Aleta and her mom need to cut off of a board to get a shorter board?

Preparation

Finally, school was out for the summer. The days were getting warmer, and best of all, the trees in the yard had lots of nearly ripe lemons! Aleta decided it was time to buy sugar and cups for the stand.

Aleta's parents loaned her the money to buy sugar and cups. She bought the 5-pound bag of sugar for $3.99, and the package of cups for $5.00. The store charged 6% sales tax on the cups, but not the sugar.

What was the total cost of the cups and the sugar?

And finally, the lemons were ripe! Aleta, Marc, and Maddie learned that a ripe lemon is still very firm. A mushy citrus fruit, whether lemon, lime, or orange, was *too* ripe.

A properly ripe lemon from their trees had to be a certain size. One ripe lemon from one of their trees was about as wide as one of Marc's or Maddie's hands.

Their dad said, "When life gives you lemons, make lemonade!" as he helped them pick lemons.

Aleta responded, "I don't know about life, but our trees sure are giving us lemons!"

 What's the Word?

Aleta's dad used the proverb, "When life gives you lemons, make lemonade." A proverb is a brief and clever statement that communicates life wisdom. Perhaps you have tasted a slice of raw lemon or sipped pure lemon juice. Lemons are very sour, but the sweetness of sugar lets most people enjoy the flavor of lemons, as in lemonade. So a less poetic way to restate this proverb may be, "When life hands you something less than pleasant, make the most of it."

CONNECTING TO HISTORY

Lemonade is a very popular drink in North America as well as other parts of the world. Lemons are also an important ingredient in Mediterranean and Arabic cooking. What do we know about lemons and lemonade?

The origin of the lemon tree is a bit of a mystery. The plant seems to have originated in Asia. It grew in areas that are now northern Burma, Assam in southern India, and part of southern China. Eventually, lemon trees were brought across Persia and the Arab world to the Mediterranean. A similar citrus fruit, called the citron, was already known in the Middle East and Mediterranean regions in ancient times. Citrons are generally larger than lemons. And they have a thicker rind and less juice and pulp.

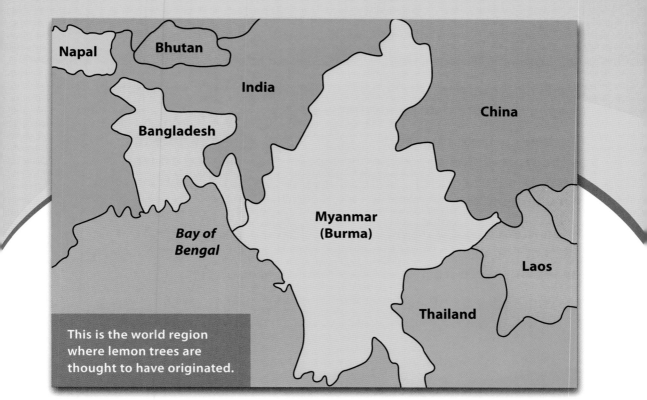

This is the world region where lemon trees are thought to have originated.

Lemon trees appeared further west during the time of Ancient Rome. They were first used as ornamental garden plants in Persia and other areas of the Middle East. Between 1000 and 1150, the lemon tree became widely cultivated throughout the Mediterranean region and the Arab world.

The earliest written account of lemonade is from medieval Egypt, in the 1300s. We know from writings of the medieval Persian poet Nasir-i-Khusraw and records of the Jewish community in medieval Cairo that people used lemons. By the year 1104, lemon juice mixed with lots of sugar was a popular local drink. It was also commonly traded to other countries. The sugar used may have been made from fruits of the date palm. The drink was called *qatarmizat*, and it seems to be the origin of what we know as lemonade.

Open for Business

One Friday morning, Aleta picked a few more lemons and got ready to open the lemonade stand that weekend.

The lemons from their trees yielded about the same amount of juice as the store-bought lemons had. So, they still needed 16 lemons per batch. In all, they had picked enough lemons for 3.5 batches. How many lemons did they harvest?

When Aleta first calculated how much profit she could earn with one batch of lemonade, she had included the price of lemons. Now that the lemons were free, she calculated her profit again.

She could save $3.60 per batch by using lemons from their trees.

There is a 6% sales tax on cups.

$$\$1.60 \times 0.06 = \$0.10$$
$$\$1.60 + \$0.10 = \$1.70$$

So, the new cost per batch was:

Sugar	$0.36
+ Cups	$1.70
	$2.06

Say Aleta earns $8.00 for each batch of lemonade she sells. Now, subtract the new cost for making each batch. What is Aleta's per-batch profit?

The next day, Aleta started juicing lemons. Marc and Maddie took the poster board and a marker and made a sign, which their mom helped attach to the stand.

By noon, they had everything set up and ready to go! Their very first customer was Aleta's good friend, Naomi.

They sold most of their first batch in about an hour and a half. Pooka joined the scene and knocked over the last bit of lemonade. They decided to call it a day.

They sold 15 servings at $0.50 per serving. How much money did Aleta, Marc, and Maddie collect on their first day of the lemonade stand?

Everyone was a bit tired from their first day of work. But they were determined to sell more lemonade the next day. With help from her dad and Maddie, Aleta prepared one full batch in the late morning.

This time they sold all 16 servings! They ran out of lemonade quickly. So, Aleta decided that they would make more than one batch each day the following weekend.

After two days of sales, they had sold a total of 31 servings and collected a total of $15.50.

Aleta wanted to pay her parents back $11.41 for the supplies they had used.

How much will Aleta have left if she pays her parents what she owes them?

MATH AT WORK

Running a lemonade stand is similar to running a restaurant. People in both businesses have to know how to work with money. Both businesses have start-up costs, because ingredients must be purchased before food or drinks can be served.

And, someone has to collect money from the customers and often give change. Unlike owners of a lemonade stand, restaurant owners charge sales tax on the food and drink they serve to their customers. A restaurant owner, of course, has far more expenses than the owner of a lemonade stand. A professional business owner has to pay for utilities like electricity and water, pay employees, and pay income taxes on their profits.

In any kind of business, however, unexpected things can happen. Food prices can change. Sometimes there are fewer customers than expected. At other times, there are more. Restaurant owners learn quickly how to deal with unexpected problems.

Summer Hours

As the next weekend approached, Aleta realized that they were already getting low on cups for the lemonade stand! And they would have to pick more lemons. The neighborhood pool was a short walk away, and it was scheduled to open that weekend. Families would be walking by the stand all day. So, Aleta expected to sell a lot more lemonade this weekend.

The cups were on sale, so she bought two packages for $8.50. With 6% sales tax, what was the total cost of the new cups? How will you find out?

Traffic to and from the neighborhood pool made a big difference at the lemonade stand. Aleta and her family prepared four batches of lemonade in all, and sold 59 servings over two days! Their uncle and aunt also donated a dozen muffins to sell at the stand. Aleta sold these for 25¢ each.

All together, Aleta collected $32.50 over the second weekend. She gave her parents $9.01 to pay them back for the new cups. How much profit did Aleta, Marc, and Maddie make their second weekend?

After paying expenses, their profit from the first weekend was $4.09. What was the profit from the lemonade stand after the first two weekends?

The next weekend that Aleta, Marc, and Maddie made and sold lemonade, the weather was overcast. Fewer people went to the pool, and fewer people were out and about. They had fewer customers at the lemonade stand, but they still sold some lemonade, and another dozen muffins that their aunt and uncle had made for them.

The weekend after that, the sun came back out and the hot summer weather really set in. Almost no one wanted muffins, but a lot of people wanted lemonade! One customer asked if they were thinking of making pink lemonade sometime. Aleta and Marc laughed. Aleta said, no, they weren't planning to.

Over these two weekends, they sold 86 servings of lemonade and some more muffins. They continued to charge $0.50 per serving. What was their total amount in sales of lemonade over these two weekends?

Home Stretch

Sales at the lemonade stand continued to go up and down. On some days they sold less. On others, they sold a lot more. On days when they sold less, they ended up drinking the leftovers. As the summer wore on, they were getting to like lemonade less and less.

One morning Maddie observed that there were fewer lemons on their trees. All along, Aleta had been adding their sales carefully and recording what they spent on supplies. Fewer lemons wouldn't be a problem. By the time they ran out of lemons altogether, Aleta was sure that they would have what they needed—money to buy birthday presents for Grandma.

One evening when they weren't selling lemonade, Grandma stopped by to visit.

"I want to get some lemons from your trees. I didn't have many this year, and I want to make lemonade for my birthday party." But when Grandma looked in Aleta's backyard, she paused. "Oh, you didn't get many lemons this year either."

Aleta looked at her parents. Marc and Maddie looked at each other. No one said a word. Even Pooka was silent. Suddenly, Grandma changed the subject. "Now, let's talk about birthday cake!" she said.

Everyone began chattering about their favorite cake flavors, and lemons were forgotten.

The summer was almost over. The new school year was growing ever closer. And Grandma's birthday party was coming up fast. But Aleta knew they had earned enough to give Grandma some special birthday presents.

By selling 216 servings of lemonade and several dozen muffins over summer weekends, they had made a total of $116.25.

Their total costs for supplies and ingredients were $35.36.

What was the total profit from the lemonade stand?

Gifts for Grandma

Aleta, Marc, and Maddie counted their profits once more. "Wow!" Marc exclaimed. "That's a lot of money!"

"You're right," Aleta said. "Now we have enough to buy our gifts for Grandma."

Dad drove everyone to an art store to pick out frames. Marc wanted a frame for the great picture his mom had taken of the three of them working at the lemonade stand.

Aleta wanted a frame for the black-and-white picture of Grandma at a lemonade stand that she had found in the scrapbook.

And Maddie wanted a frame for a colorful paper collage that she had made just for Grandma.

The three picture frames came to a total of $70.00. Aleta thought she could almost calculate the amount of sales tax in her head. With 6% sales tax added, how much did they pay for the three picture frames?

The Final Ingredients

Finally, it was Grandma's birthday. Lots of family members came to celebrate. Grandma enjoyed the framed pictures. She laughed when she saw the black-and-white one.

On the table with the cake, fruit, and other snacks, Aleta, Marc, and Mattie found a pitcher of pink lemonade. Marc looked at it suspiciously.

"Grandma, did you make the pink lemonade yourself?"

It turns out she had. Maddie asked her what made it pink.

"Well, my grandmother used to put beet juice in to make it pink. But I like to add raspberry juice."

"Better than pink tights," Maddie whispered to Aleta.

"Sounds good to me!" Aleta said to her Grandma. "I'll pour all of us a cup!"

Aleta was tired when they got home from the party. The summer was at an end. So was the lemonade stand. The lemonade stand had been a lot of work, and mostly interesting. But she was ready for school to start again.

But she had one last small piece of business to take care of. She was sitting in the living room when Pooka the cat wandered in.

"I'm so glad you wandered in here," she said to the cat. "I was too tired to come find you. Remember all that lemonade we made and sold all summer long? We had a little bit left and got you something. It cost $4.40 plus tax, which totaled . . . oh, never mind! Here, Pooka."

Aleta's business idea had been successful. And, she had learned some good business lessons. Next summer, she thought, she'd expand her business. She'd spend the next school year thinking about it.

The morning after her Grandma's birthday party, Aleta received an e-mail.

Gina: I need help!

Aleta: What do you need?

Gina: My friends and I are planning a bake sale for the first day of school. I need help with some math!

Aleta: Your timing is perfect. I ran my own business all summer. I can definitely help you!

Gina: Great! I have a great cupcake recipe. I need 5 times more cupcakes than the recipe makes. I know how to multiply the measurements in the recipe by 5. But I need help multiplying money amounts. How do I figure out how much the ingredients will cost?

Aleta: First, find the total cost of the flour, sugar, and other ingredients. Include the cost of paper cupcake cups, too. What's the total?

Gina: I can use the flour and sugar we have in our kitchen. But the frosting and paper cups cost $2.79.

Aleta: Okay. You want to make 5 times more cupcakes, so you need to multiply the total cost by 5. There are different ways you can do that. Do you want to know about all of them?"

Gina: "Absolutely!" Aleta wrote a long response:

Idea 1: Remember that the place values to the right of the decimal point represent a fraction, or parts of a whole. So, you can **rewrite a decimal number as a fraction.**

And you can rewrite any whole number as a fraction without changing its value. Just give it a denominator of 1.

So, you would write your problem as $\frac{279}{100} \times \frac{5}{1}$. When you find the answer, you rewrite the fraction as a decimal.

Rewriting decimal numbers as fractions and then back again is easy, but it takes time. Plus, if the numerator is large, dividing the numerator by the denominator can be challenging. So, you might want to choose a faster way to multiply.

Idea 2: You can use **partial products** to multiply 2.79 by 5. This is a great way to understand how multiplication of decimal numbers works, and to check for mistakes at the same time. But this also takes extra time. This doesn't seem useful for getting a quick answer.

Idea 3: You could use the **Distributive Property** to multiply. It takes time to use this method, and sometimes, it gets complicated if the numbers are large. So, once again, you might not find this the easiest or fastest way to find the total cost.

Idea 4: I would use an **algorithm** for multiplying decimal numbers.

Aleta sent the e-mail and waited. Gina's answer came in seconds.

Gina: Let's use this way. Walk me through it, will you?

Aleta wrote back: Don't worry about the decimal point at first. First, multiply the ones. You'll need to **regroup**. That means that you have so many ones after multiplying that you can make four new groups of ten. So, write a 4 above the tens place.

$$\begin{array}{r} 4 \\ 2.79 \\ \times \quad 5 \\ \hline 5 \end{array}$$

Next, multiply the tens. Regroup tens this time.

$$\begin{array}{r} 3\ 4 \\ 2.79 \\ \times \quad 5 \\ \hline 95 \end{array}$$

Then, multiply the hundreds. Regroup the hundreds into one group of one thousand and 3 groups of one hundred.

$$\begin{array}{r} 3\ 4 \\ 2.79 \\ \times \quad 5 \\ \hline 1395 \end{array}$$

Count the total number of decimal places in both factors. Start to the right of the product and count that many places back. Put in the decimal point. Got it?

Gina: Got it! There are two decimal places. So, the total cost is $13.95.

Aleta: Exactly!

Gina: Thanks! I owe you some cupcakes!

WHAT COMES NEXT?

Do you know anyone who owns his or her own business? Do you have any interest in running your own business some day?

For any business, many calculations are figured out using a calculator, computer program, or cash register. But it's still very important to understand the mathematics concepts involved in business calculations.

Interview someone you know who either runs his or her own business or works in some way with money in a business where he or she is employed.

Think about what the business is, and ask your acquaintance some questions like the following:

- How often do you work with money amounts?
- What if any calculations do you do mentally? In writing?
- What kinds of supplies do you have to order in multiple quantities?
- Do you have to charge customers sales tax for your products or services?

There are probably a lot of matters related to running a business that you haven't imagined. Invite the person you are interviewing to ask you questions. Learn all you can. It will be useful to you when you begin thinking about a summer business of your own.

GLOSSARY

addends: the numbers you add in an addition problem.

algorithm: a step-by-step process for a calculation.

base ten system: a system of writing numbers in which each digit has a value ten times that of a digit to its right.

decimal number: a number containing a decimal point.

decimal point: a dot separating the whole number from the parts of a whole in a decimal number.

denominator: the number of equal parts into which a whole is divided, shown as the number below the line in a fraction.

Distributive Property: The product of a number and a sum, such as $(x \times [a + b])$, is equal to the sum of individual products of the number and the addends, or $([x \times a] + [x \times b])$.

estimate: to guess or make a rough calculation. Usually, a person who estimates has enough information to come close to an actual amount.

factor: the numbers you multiply in a multiplication problem.

ingredient: the things that go into a recipe, such as flour, sugar, and water.

numerator: the number of equal parts described by a fraction, shown as the number above the line in a fraction.

operation: an action such as addition, subtraction, multiplication, and division of numbers.

partial product: in multiplication, the product of one number and one place value in the number it is being multiplied by.

place value: the value of a digit, determined by its place in a number.

product: the result of multiplying two numbers.

profit: difference between the amount earned and the amount spent in producing something.

recipe: a set of instructions you follow to make something such as a pitcher of fresh lemonade.

regroup: to use place value to think of numbers in different ways, such as thinking of 1 ten as 10 ones.

FURTHER READING

FICTION

Crunch, by Leslie Connor, Katherine Tegen Books, 2010

NONFICTION

Better Than a Lemonade Stand!: Small Business Ideas for Kids, by Daryl Bernstein, Aladdin/Beyond Words, 2012

Starting a Business: Have Fun and Make Money, by Carla Mooney, Norwood House Press, 2011

ADDITIONAL NOTES

The page references below provide answers to questions asked throughout the book. Questions whose answers will vary are not addressed.

Page 6: $\frac{69}{10} = 6\frac{9}{10}$ pounds = 6.9 pounds

Page 7: 8.74 pounds

Page 8: $(0.06 \times 3) + (0.06 \times 0.8) + (0.06 \times 0.05) = (0.18) + (0.048) + (0.003) = 0.231$, or $0.23; $3.80 + $0.23 = $4.08

Page 9: $2.3 \times 3 = 6.9$ pounds

Page 13: 1.1 lbs. × $0.80/lb. = $0.88, or 88¢

Page 14: $1.1 \times 4 = 4.4$ pounds

Page 15: $(4 \times 0.8) + (0.4 \times 0.8) = 3.2 + 0.32 = $3.52

Page 17: $2.00 × 0.06 = $0.12; $2.00 + $0.12 = $2.12

Page 18: Yes; $0.36 × 11 = $3.96, which is close to the full bag of sugar, $3.99.

Page 19: $5.00 × 0.06 = $0.30; $5.00 + $0.30 = $5.30

Page 20: 16 × $0.50 = $8.00; $8.00 − $5.00 = $3.00 profit

Page 21: $1.60 × 0.06 = about 0.10. $3.52 + $0.36 + $1.60 + $0.10 = $5.58

Page 23: $2.50

Page 25: 0.47 m, or 47 cm

Page 26: $5.30 + 3.99 = $9.29

Page 30: $3.5 \times 16 = 56$ lemons; $8.00 − $2.06 = $5.94

Page 31: 15 × $0.50 = $7.50

Page 32: $15.50 − $11.41 = $4.09

Page 34: $8.50 + $0.51 = $9.01

Page 35: $32.50 − $9.01 = $23.49; $4.09 + $23.49 = $27.58

Page 36: 86 × $0.50 = $43.00

Page 38: $116.25 − $35.36 = $80.89

Page 39: $70.00 × 0.06 = $4.20; $70.00 + $4.20 = $74.20

INDEX

CONTENT CONSULTANT

David T. Hughes

David is an experienced mathematics teacher, writer, presenter, and adviser. He serves as a consultant for the Partnership for Assessment of Readiness for College and Careers. David has also worked as the Senior Program Coordinator for the Charles A. Dana Center at The University of Texas at Austin and was an editor and contributor for the *Mathematics Standards in the Classroom* series.